DIGITAL DECEPTION

DIGITAL DECEPTION
When Online Friends Become Real-Life Nightmares

Michael-Paul Huling

DEDICATION

To Orion, Aurora, and Liliana.

Table of Contents

Chapter 1: The First Connection

Nathan Williams was the kind of kid who knew every corner of every playground in East Greenwich, Rhode Island where he lived. At 12, he was energetic, smart, and as his mother Alyssa often remarked, "too clever for his own good." His bedroom, a sanctuary lined with science fiction posters and shelves crammed with baseball cards and superhero comics, reflected his vibrant and curious spirit.

It was late on a Thursday afternoon when Nathan's life took a virtual turn. School had just let out for the weekend, and he was at his locker when he overheard some older kids talking about the latest video game to capture the attention of children all over the country; Craftworld. Intrigued by their enthusiastic chatter about building worlds and cooperative adventures, Nathan's imagination ignited. By the time he walked through the front door of his house, he had made up his mind to download the game.

"Mom, I'm home!" he called out, dropping his backpack and football by the entrance and making a beeline for his bedroom.

His mother, working from her home office, poked her head out, her expression a mix of welcome and warning. "Hi, honey. Homework first, okay? And remember what we said about screen time."

"Sure, Mom," Nathan replied, his voice the epitome of innocence. He did intend to do his homework. Eventually. But first, he had a new world to explore, and he couldn't wait!

Upstairs in his room, he fired up his laptop and began installing Craftworld. Nathan's social media accounts were already buzzing from the hilarious memes he frequently shared, earning him a fair bit of popularity at school. But as he clicked on the Craftworld installer, he felt like he was stepping into a whole new level of cool.

The game loaded, and Nathan created his avatar with an excitement that made his hands tremble slightly. He chose a bright red t-shirt and jeans for his character, a digital version of his favorite outfit, and plunged into the vast expanse of Craftworld. The game was everything the older kids had hyped it up to be and more. Nathan was hooked.

For the next hour, he explored the digital terrain, marveling at the landscapes that stretched endlessly in every direction. He dug into mountains, swam across rivers, and even started building a small fort. It was during this construction project that he first noticed another player walking by named Nicodemus74.

"Need some help?" The message popped up in the chat window on the bottom left of his screen.

Nathan hesitated. He knew the rules—no talking to strangers online, always be cautious. But this was different, right? This was just a game. He typed back, "Sure, thanks!"

Nicodemus74 was quick to respond, guiding Nathan through the crafting of better tools and the secrets of faster building. His new friend seemed to know everything about Craftworld, and Nathan was impressed.

"You're really good at this," Nathan typed, watching as Nicodemus74 expertly laid down blocks.

"Thanks! Been playing since the beta. How old are you?" Nicodemus74 asked.

Nathan paused, his fingers hovering over the keys. He remembered his mom's warning about sharing personal information. "I'm 12. How about you?"

"Same here!" came the reply. That was all Nathan needed to lower his guard just a bit more. They continued playing, and as they did, Nathan shared little bits about his life, the recent excitement of his twin siblings, Olivia and Oliver, learning to drive, and his father's frequent business trips for his job in pharmaceutical sales.

As the sky outside his window shifted from blue to shades of orange and pink, Nathan heard his mother calling him for dinner. He promised Nicodemus74 he'd be back online later and shut down his laptop.

At the dinner table, Nathan was unusually quiet, lost in thought about his new friend and the vast digital world they could explore together.

"Everything okay, Nate?" his mother asked, watching her son push his food around his plate.

"Yeah, everything's great! I made a new friend today," Nathan said, his face lighting up with a smile.

"That's wonderful, honey. Where did you meet?" his mother was always interested in her children's lives, her questions gentle but attentive.

"In Craftworld," Nathan replied, and then hurriedly added, seeing his mother's frown, "But it's okay, he's my age and we're just talking about the game!"

His mother's frown deepened slightly. "Just remember what we talked about, Nate. It's important to be careful with who you meet online. Not everyone is who they say they are."

Nathan nodded, though inside, he felt a twinge of annoyance. He wasn't a little kid anymore, after all. He knew how to handle a game. But out of respect for his mom, whom he sometimes teasingly called "brah" to her chagrin, he simply said, "I know, Mom. I'll be careful."

Later that night, back in his room, Nathan logged into Craftworld again. Nicodemus74 was already there, waiting.

"Ready for another adventure?" Nicodemus74 asked.

"Always!" Nathan typed back.

As they played, Nathan felt the real world slip away, replaced by the exciting possibilities of Craftworld. Unbeknownst to him, this was just the beginning of a journey that would teach him more about the digital world than he ever wanted to know.

Chapter 2: A Virtual Bond

The sun was just beginning to set, casting a warm orange glow through Nathan's bedroom window. Outside, the neighborhood kids were gathering for an evening game of touch football, their shouts and laughter drifting up to him. Yet, inside, Nathan sat at his computer, his attention fully captured by the glowing screen in front of him. Craftworld had become his new playground, and within this digital landscape, he found adventure and camaraderie that seemed just as real as the games he played outside.

Over the past few weeks, Nathan's daily routine had subtly shifted. After school, he'd rush home, bypassing the usual stops at the park or the corner store with his friends, and head straight to his room. He'd sit down at his laptop, eager to log into Craftworld and meet up with Nicodemus74. His mother had noticed the change, her gentle reminders about homework and outdoor play becoming more frequent. However, Nathan engrossed in his virtual world, found it easy to nod along without really listening.

"Remember, moderation is key," his mother would say, a hint of concern lacing her voice as she passed by his open door. Nathan would offer a quick "Yeah, Mom, I know," his eyes never leaving the screen.

One evening, as Nathan was deeply engrossed in a particularly challenging quest, his brother Oliver walked in. "Still on this game, huh?" he remarked, leaning against the doorframe with a half-amused, half-disapproving smirk.

Nathan jumped slightly, caught off guard. "Just finishing up this level," he lied smoothly, minimizing the game window to show an open homework document.

Oliver raised an eyebrow but shrugged. "Don't let Mom catch you. You know how she feels about you being glued to that thing." He was more laid-back than their mother about rules, and though he saw Nathan's fixation, he didn't think much of it beyond typical pre-teen obsession.

"Thanks, Ollie. I'll be done soon, promise," Nathan assured him, and with a conspiratorial grin, Oliver left the room, leaving Nathan to dive back into the world of Craftworld.

That night, Nathan and Nicodemus74 embarked on an epic quest together to defeat the notorious Doom Dragon, a beast that had eluded Nathan several times before. With Nicodemus74's guidance, Nathan learned new strategies and crafted the special weapons needed to take it down once and for all. The thrill of the hunt and the shared victory when they finally slayed the dragon deepened Nathan's appreciation for his new friend.

"You're a natural at this," Nicodemus74 typed, as they stood atop the virtual mountain, watching the sun rise over the blocky horizon of Craftworld.

"Couldn't have done it without you," Nathan replied, feeling a surge of gratitude. The game wasn't just about adventure; it was about connection.

As they ventured back to their home base to store their loot, the conversation turned more personal. Nicodemus74 shared stories about his own school and friends, which sounded remarkably similar to Nathan's experiences. Nathan found himself opening up about his day-to-day life, discussing school projects, his favorite subjects, and even his frustrations with being the youngest sibling.

"You get me," Nathan typed one evening, a smile playing on his lips as he read Nicodemus74's sympathetic response to a story about Oliver borrowing his favorite hoodie without asking.

"Yeah, it's like we're leading parallel lives," Nicodemus74 replied. The ease of their exchanges made Nathan feel like he was chatting with a friend he had known all his life, not just a few weeks.

Their sessions in Craftworld became the highlight of Nathan's day. He looked forward to logging in, not just for the game itself but for the companionship it offered. Nicodemus74 was always there, like a constant in a sea of changing real-world dynamics.

One weekend, while his family was busy with various activities—Oliver and Olivia attended a local music festival in Newport, and his father working late—Nathan spent hours on Craftworld. He and Nicodemus74 explored new territories, built elaborate structures, and shared countless tips and tricks. The game became their secret clubhouse, a place where they could talk freely and escape the pressures of everyday life.

However, as Nathan's virtual life flourished, his real-life connections began to suffer. He missed a couple of martial arts lessons, and his school friends started to notice his absence at their usual hangouts. Even his mother commented on how she missed their weekend movie nights, which had been a family tradition.

"We haven't had one in a while, Nate," his mother said one evening, a note of sadness in her voice. "Maybe this weekend we can pick something out to watch together?"

Nathan, feeling a pang of guilt, nodded. "Yeah, that sounds great, Mom."

Despite his best intentions, that weekend came and went with Nathan once again lost in Craftworld. Nicodemus74 had introduced him to a new building competition on an elite server, and the excitement of the event swept away any thoughts of movie nights or spending time with his family.

As Nathan lay in bed that Sunday night, his room dark except for the soft glow of his alarm clock, he felt a twinge of regret. He realized he had barely spoken to his family all weekend. *It's just this one time,* he rationalized, trying to shake off the guilt. But deep down, he knew his priorities had shifted more than he wanted to admit.

The bond he formed with Nicodemus74 was strong, filled with shared secrets and digital triumphs. Yet, as he drifted off to sleep, Nathan couldn't help but wonder if he was missing out on more than he gained in his quest for virtual victories. As much as he valued his friendship with Nicodemus74, the growing distance between him and his real-world friends and family was becoming harder to ignore.

Chapter 3: Small Revelations

As autumn crept into the small town of East Greenwich, the leaves began their fiery transformation, and with the change of seasons came a deepening of Nathan's friendship with Nicodemus74. Their daily exchanges in Craftworld had become as routine as the school bell or dinner at six. However, as their virtual world expanded, so too did the nature of their conversations, inching ever closer to the boundaries Nathan's mother had warned him about.

One crisp evening, as Nathan wrapped himself in a blanket at his desk, the glow of his screen illuminating his focused expression, Nicodemus74's questions began to probe a little deeper.

"Hey, what school do you go to again?" Nicodemus74 typed into the chat, his avatar pausing in the middle of constructing a new building in their shared space.

Nathan hesitated for a moment. He knew he shouldn't share too much, but the casual way Nico asked made it seem like just another piece of harmless chatter between friends. "East Greenwich Middle," Nathan replied, adding quickly, "It's pretty average, but I like it okay."

"Cool, cool. Do you hang out with a lot of friends there?" Nicodemus74 asked, his avatar resuming its task.

"Yeah, a bunch. We play football during recess mostly," Nathan typed back, his fingers hesitating slightly on the keys before continuing. "But I haven't seen them much outside of school lately. Been too caught up in here."

"Yeah, I get that. It's the same for me. Craftworld's way more fun than real stuff sometimes," Nicodemus74 responded. There was a pause before he added, "Got any siblings?"

Nathan smiled, typing more freely now. "Yeah, older twins, Olivia and Oliver. They're sixteen. Just started driving. It's been chaos," he laughed, the sound echoing slightly in his room.

"Twins, huh? That's gotta be interesting. Bet they keep your parents busy," Nicodemus74 mused.

"Definitely. They're cool though. We get into all sorts of trouble together." As Nathan shared these snippets of his life, it didn't occur to him that he was slowly painting a detailed picture of his family and their routines. In his mind, he was just chatting with a friend, someone who understood and shared his world.

Their conversation shifted back to the game, discussing strategies for an upcoming Craftworld PVP tournament. As they planned, Nicodemus74's questions weaved seamlessly between game tactics and personal anecdotes. Nathan found himself sharing more about his daily life, mentioning how his father often traveled for work, leaving him more time to play online, or how his mother's home office was right next to his room, filled with gadgets and tech stuff for her job.

"Your mom works with tech? That's cool," Nicodemus74 typed, his avatar stopping to face Nathan's.

"Yeah, she's a product manager. She's always on her computer. I've picked up a lot just from listening to her talk," Nathan replied, a trace of pride in his voice.

"That's really cool, man. You must know a lot about computers then," Nicodemus74 said, sounding impressed.

"Sort of," Nathan admitted. "Still learning, but it's interesting."

As their game session drew to a close that night, Nathan didn't think much of the conversation. To him, it was just another evening spent with a good friend. However, as he shut down his laptop and crawled into bed, a small voice in the back of his mind whispered a warning. He pushed it aside, attributing it to the overcautious warnings of his mother. Nico was his friend and he trusted him.

In the following days, the pattern continued. Each session with Nico seemed to peel back another layer of Nathan's life. School projects, favorite hangouts, even his recent birthday party—the details spilled out as easily as talk of Craftworld strategies. Nicodemus74 was always there, always interested, always asking just the right questions to keep the conversation flowing.

One day, as Nathan shared a funny incident from school, Nicodemus74's response came with a slight delay. "Man, wish I could've seen that. Bet it was hilarious."

"Yeah, it was epic. You should've seen the look on Mrs. Mercurio's face!" Nathan chuckled as he typed, completely at ease.

"Hey, you ever think about what it'd be like to meet up for real? Just hang out, play some football?" Nicodemus74 asked casually, almost too casually.

Nathan paused, his fingers hovering over the keyboard. The question seemed innocent enough, and part of him thrilled at the idea of hanging out with his best friend from Craftworld. But another part, the part that listened to his mother's repeated cautions, hesitated.

"Maybe one day," he typed finally, a non-committal response that left him feeling both eager and uneasy.

As Nathan continued to navigate his dual worlds—the real one grounded in school and family, and the virtual one filled with dragons and deepening friendships—he remained blissfully unaware of the subtle dangers that lurked behind seemingly innocent questions. His trust in Nicodemus74 blinded him to the risks, wrapping him in a false sense of security that could, with just a few more careless words, be easily shattered.

Chapter 4: Glitches

The crisp chill of early winter settled over East Greenwich, a quiet reminder of the changing seasons. Indoors, Nathan remained nestled in the warmth of his room, his attention captured by the vibrant expanse of Craftworld. Yet, outside the virtual landscapes he cherished, troubling undercurrents began to stir, rippling through his digital life with growing persistence.

It started subtly one Saturday morning. Nathan, with a bowl of cereal beside him, logged into Craftworld to find his inventory oddly rearranged. Items he had meticulously sorted were out of place, and some resources he remembered collecting the previous night were missing from his inventory.

"Must've forgotten to save," he muttered to himself, brushing off the irregularity. He reorganized his inventory and continued playing, dismissing the incident as a slip of memory or a minor glitch in the game.

A few days later, another anomaly caught his attention. This time, it was his social media account. Nathan had a habit of sharing memes and quirky updates, which made him fairly popular among his school friends. As he scrolled through his feed, he noticed several posts and comments he did not remember making. They were harmless—more memes and a few random comments on friends' posts—but it was strange, unsettling even, that he had no recollection of posting them.

"Probably just clicked something by accident," Nathan reasoned, deleting the unfamiliar posts. The digital world was full of little bugs, he thought, and this was likely another one to add to the list.

The real unease set in later that week when Nathan received a series of emails that chilled his spine despite his attempts to rationalize them. "Password Reset Confirmation," one subject line read. He clicked on the email, his brow furrowing as he read the message thanking him for updating his password—something he had not done.

Confused, Nathan checked his other accounts linked to the same email. More emails of the same nature had flooded his inbox, each confirming changes he hadn't initiated. A lump formed in his throat, the first real wave of panic setting in. Still, he tried to stay calm, attributing the emails to possible mistakes or a mix-up from the service providers.

"It's just a glitch," he told himself, resetting the passwords back to what they were and activating two-factor authentication on his accounts, a safety measure he had heard his mother mention in passing.

Despite his efforts to secure his accounts, the unsettling incidents didn't stop. A few nights later, while Nathan was deep in a Craftworld session, his game suddenly logged out. An error message flashed on the screen: "You have been logged out because your account is currently active on another device."

Nathan stared at the message, his heart racing. He tried to log back in, but his password no longer worked. Frantically, he went through the password recovery process, his mind racing with possibilities. Someone was meddling with his digital life, but why? And how?

Once he regained access to his game account, Nathan found changes that couldn't be ignored. His avatar was dressed differently, and his home base was modified in ways that he would never have done. It felt personal, a violation of his digital sanctuary.

In the game's chat, a message from Nicodemus74 popped up, "Everything okay?"

"Yeah, just some weird glitches happening," Nathan typed back, trying to sound nonchalant, though his fingers trembled slightly as he typed.

"Strange stuff. Let me know if you need help fixing anything," Nicodemus74 offered, his words meant to be reassuring.

"Thanks, I think I've got it," Nathan replied, his trust in his online friend still intact, not connecting the disturbances in his digital world with the person on the other side of their conversations.

As Nathan logged off that night, the reality of his situation hadn't fully sunk in. He lay in bed, the glow from his laptop casting shadows across his room, his mind a whirl of confusion and fear. These weren't just minor glitches. Someone was tampering with his digital life, manipulating his online presence, and invading his privacy.

But the gravity of these breaches, the potential dangers lurking behind each unauthorized login and password reset, remained obscured to Nathan, cloaked under his naive belief in coincidences and minor technical faults. The digital world he loved was turning against him, and he was unprepared for the storm that was quietly brewing on the horizon.

Chapter 5: The Invasion Begins

The Williams household was always lively, filled with the typical chaos of a family of five. However, a new kind of disorder began to seep into their lives, one that was unfamiliar and deeply unsettling. It started innocently enough, with Nathan's older sister Olivia receiving a strange phone call on her cell phone one evening while the family was enjoying dinner. Spaghetti and homemade meatballs. Nathan's favorite!

"Who was it?" their mother asked, noting the puzzled expression on her daughter's face as she hung up.

"Some prank callers, I guess," Olivia shrugged it off. "They just asked if I was happy with my insurance policy and then hung up."

"But you don't have any insurance policies," Oliver pointed out, a forkful of spaghetti paused mid-air.

"I know, right? Weird," Olivia replied, pushing the incident to the back of her mind.

However, the oddities didn't stop there. Over the next few days, more mysterious occurrences piled up. Bills for expensive gadgets none of them had ordered arrived in the mail, and Nathan's mother started receiving notifications about a credit card application submitted under her name. Each piece of mail felt like a brick adding weight to an invisible burden the family hadn't noticed accumulating.

Meanwhile, Nathan was wrestling with his own growing unease. He had noticed more anomalies in his digital life—posts he didn't make appearing on his social media, friends responding to messages he hadn't sent. It all spiraled into a constant buzz of anxiety, which he tried desperately to silence. Fearful of his mother's reaction and the potential repercussions of admitting he might have compromised their security, he remained silent.

One particularly troubling evening, as Nathan lay in bed, the gravity of the situation became too heavy to bear alone. He picked up his phone and dialed his friend Miles, his fingers trembling slightly as he held the device to his ear.

"Hey, Miles, are you awake? I... I think I'm in trouble," Nathan's voice was a mix of fear and desperation.

"What's up?" Miles responded, his voice was groggy but concerned.

Nathan recounted the strange events, the unexplained activities on his accounts, and the unsettling changes in Craftworld. As he spoke, the pieces of a puzzle he hadn't realized he was assembling began to fall into place.

"Dude, have you been talking to anyone online? Someone new who might be doing this?" Miles asked, his tone sharpening with suspicion.

"There's just Nico... He's the only one I've really shared stuff with," Nathan admitted, a sick feeling growing in the pit of his stomach.

"Nate, think about it. It could be him. Maybe you should confront him. See if he slips up or admits to anything," Miles suggested.

The idea of confronting Nicodemus74 was daunting. He was Nathan's friend, wasn't he? Yet as the connection dawned on him,

Nathan knew what he had to do. After hanging up with Miles, he sat frozen, staring at his reflection in the dark window. His heart pounded with the realization that his trust might have been betrayed.

Gathering his courage, Nathan logged into Craftworld. His hands were cold, his fingers numb as they navigated the keyboard. He opened his inventory and drank a speed potion which helped him traverse the digital terrain swiftly, finding Nicodemus74 exactly where he expected: at their usual meeting spot by the Lake of Ancients.

Nathan's avatar approached, his digital heart pounding as palpably as his real one as he began typing... "Hey, Nico, can I ask you something?"

Nicodemus74's avatar turned to face him, dressed in a red shirt and blue jeans—exactly what Nathan usually wore. "Sure, what's up?"

"Do you know anything about some weird stuff happening to me? Like someone messing with my accounts and stuff?" Nathan typed as his anxiety continued to build up within his chest.

Nicodemus74's avatar paused, and for a moment, the digital world seemed to hold its breath. Then, a simple question hung in the air above his head, "Do you do everything Miles tells you to do?"

Nathan recoiled, his avatar stepping back involuntarily. "How would you know that?" he stammered, his fear turning to horror.

Nicodemus74 moved closer, their avatars now standing face-to-face. "I know everything about you, Nathan Williams."

The word bubble hung in the air, heavy and ominous. Nathan's heart raced, panic clawing at his throat. The digital landscape around him suddenly felt claustrophobic, threatening.

The avatar before him, once a friend, now mirrored back his deepest fears—a breach made manifest through shared confidences turned weapons.

Nathan logged off abruptly, his breaths shallow and rapid. The room was dark, the glow of the screen lingering like the echo of Nicodemus74's words. He was alone, yet he felt as if the enemy were right there in his bedroom. As he lay back in his bed, staring at the ceiling, Nathan realized the full extent of his vulnerability. The digital threads connecting him to Craftworld had woven a web that now entangled his whole family, pulling them all into an abyss of uncertainty and danger.

Chapter 6: The Unmasking of Nicodemus74

The Williams' living room, usually a place of family gatherings and movie nights, had transformed into a somber scene of official inquiry. Nathan sat on the couch, his parents, Alyssa and David, flanking him, each wearing expressions of worry and disbelief. Across from them, two federal agents from the National Cyber Investigative Joint Task Force (NCIJTF) had set up their laptops and files, their demeanor professional yet empathetic.

Agent Martinez, a seasoned investigator with sharp eyes and a reassuring voice, addressed the family. "Mr. and Mrs. Williams, Nathan, I know this has been a difficult time for your family. We're here to help. Our initial findings have uncovered quite a bit, but I need to ask a few more questions."

David Williams, normally composed, showed signs of strain. "Of course, whatever you need. We just want to get to the bottom of this."

Mrs. Williams nodded in agreement, her hands tightly clasped together. "Yes, please."

Agent Martinez turned to Nathan. "Nathan, when did you first notice something was wrong with your accounts and social media?"

Nathan swallowed, the weight of the situation pressing down on him. "It started with small things. My game account had items moved around, and then I saw posts I didn't make on social media. But I didn't think much of it at first. I thought they were just glitches."

"And when did you share personal information with Nicodemus74?" the other agent, Agent Lee, asked, her tone gentle yet firm.

Nathan hesitated, glancing at his parents before replying, "A few weeks after we started playing together. He seemed like just a kid like me... I told him about my school, my family, things like that."

Agent Martinez nodded, making notes. "With the information you provided in your initial complaint and a brief scan of your son's laptop, we were able to trace the digital footprints left by the Craftworld username Nicodemus74. It appears that this individual is likely a known cybercriminal named Wade Allen Burgess. He's not a child; he's an adult who has served time for similar offenses and is on the FBI's wanted list."

The room went silent as the gravity of the deception sank in. Mrs. William's voice trembled as she spoke, "How could he do this? Pretend to be a child?"

"It's a common tactic among predators," Agent Martinez explained. "They create trust and then exploit it. In this case, Burgess used the information Nathan provided to access your family's financial accounts and personal data."

David rubbed his forehead, the stress evident in his voice. "What's the extent of the damage?"

Agent Lee answered, "Unfortunately, it's significant. As you know, your bank accounts have been drained and credit cards were maxed out, but it appears several loans were taken out in both of your names without your knowledge. And that's just the tip of the iceberg. Our team is working with your bank and credit agencies to mitigate the damage, but it will take time to resolve."

The agents then detailed how Burgess operated through the dark web and was currently believed to be in Ecuador, making apprehension difficult. They reassured the Williams family that they were doing everything possible to track him down and prevent further incidents.

After the agents left, the family sat in stunned silence. Nathan felt a mix of anger and guilt, his initial trust in Nicodemus74 now a source of deep regret.

"I'm so sorry, Mom, Dad," Nathan finally said, his voice barely above a whisper. "I didn't know. I thought he was my friend."

As the reality of the breach settled over the Williams' living room, Nathan's father abruptly stood up, his chair scraping back sharply against the hardwood floor. With a heavy sigh, he stormed off into the kitchen, the sound of his footsteps echoing in his distress. The atmosphere was thick with tension, leaving Nathan and his mother sitting in an uncomfortable silence. Finally, Nathan's mother turned to him with teary eyes, her expression a mixture of disappointment and concern.

"Nathan, have you forgotten everything I've tried to teach you about online security?" Her voice was low but sharp, piercing the heavy air between them. She shook her head slowly, her next words heavy with the weight of the moment. "Go to your room, and don't think of touching any electronics tonight." Nathan nodded silently, feeling the sting of his mother's words deeper than he expected, and retreated to his room, the weight of his actions settling heavily on his shoulders.

Chapter 7: Consequences

In the days following the exposure of Nicodemus74's true identity and his criminal activities, the Williams family found themselves grappling with a cascade of repercussions. Each day brought new challenges as they worked to secure their breached accounts and restore their tarnished reputations. The physical and emotional toll was palpable, each member of the family coping in their own way. Nathan's father spent hours on the phone with banks and credit agencies, while his mother meticulously reviewed every account and subscription, ensuring no stone was left unturned in their quest to reclaim their digital lives.

Nathan, however, faced a different kind of fallout. At school, whispers followed him down the hallways, and stares pinned him to the wall like a specimen under scrutiny. The malicious posts that had appeared under his social media accounts—crafted by Burgess but bearing Nathan's name—had sown confusion and mistrust among his classmates. Some were hurtful, others just bewildering, but all of them painted a picture of a Nathan that was unrecognizable to his friends.

One chilly morning, as Nathan retrieved books from his locker, he overheard a group of students snickering nearby. "Hey, there's the meme lord, bet he's hacked our accounts too," one of them jeered. Nathan slammed his locker shut, a flush of embarrassment coloring his cheeks. He wanted to shout, to explain it wasn't him, but the words tangled up in his throat, and he walked away, his head bowed.

In the cafeteria, the isolation was even more pronounced. Where he used to sit surrounded by friends, there was now an empty space around him, as if his presence was something to be avoided. He missed the laughter and the shared jokes that didn't come at his expense. The realization that his virtual actions—or those impersonated by someone else—had real-world implications was a harsh lesson.

Nathan's mother noticed the change in her son. One evening, she found Nathan sitting alone in his room, not on his computer, but staring out the window. The vibrant spirit he once radiated seemed dimmed.

"Nathan," she began softly, sitting beside him. "I know it's hard right now, but it's going to get better."

Nathan looked at her, his eyes searching for assurance in her words. "But what if it doesn't? What if they keep believing I did those things?"

Nathan's mother took her son's hand, squeezing it gently. "We're fixing things one step at a time. And we're doing it together. But you need to talk to your friends, explain what happened. They'll understand, Nathan. They know you."

Bolstered by his mother's encouragement, Nathan decided to face the issue head-on. The next day at school, he approached his classmates during lunch, his nerves jittery but resolved to clear his name.

"Hey, guys," he started, his voice steady despite the butterflies in his stomach. "I want to explain something about those weird posts and messages from my account."

He laid it all out—the game, Nicodemus74, Wade Allen Burgess, the identity theft. His friends listened, their expressions shifting from suspicion to surprise as they began to grasp the situation.

"So, you didn't send those weird messages?" one friend asked, skepticism lingering.

"No, it was all him—Burgess. He hacked into everything," Nathan explained, his relief noticeable as understanding dawned on their faces.

The conversation marked a turning point. While not everything returned to normal immediately, the ice began to melt. Apologies were made, and slowly, laughter returned to Nathan's lunch table.

Back at home, as the family's digital integrity gradually restored, they invested time in strengthening their online security practices. Nathan's dad installed new, robust security software on all devices, while his mother organized a family meeting to discuss online safety and privacy.

"We all need to be more careful about what we share online," Nathan's father said, leading the discussion. "It's not just about avoiding viruses or hackers; it's about protecting our family."

Nathan listened, truly listened, absorbing every word. The incident had unveiled the web's darker facets, revealing how deeply the virtual could entwine with the real.

Chapter 8: Lessons Learned

The whole experience was transformative for Nathan Williams. He had learned a harsh lesson in the consequences of oversharing online, a lesson that reshaped his understanding of the digital world and his role within it. As Nathan navigated the recovery process with his family, he realized that his experience could serve as a vital warning for others. Motivated by a newfound sense of responsibility, he decided to use his story to educate his peers about internet safety.

Nathan began by organizing small discussion groups at school. With the support of his teachers, he created presentations detailing his ordeal, emphasizing the importance of protecting personal information and understanding the privacy settings of online platforms. He spoke about how easily trust can be manipulated online and stressed the critical need for skepticism and vigilance in digital interactions.

His efforts soon gained momentum, and Nathan was invited to speak at other classes and even at nearby schools. Each presentation refined his message and deepened his understanding, turning him into a confident advocate for online safety. His teachers praised his initiative, and his parents beamed with pride, relieved to see him channeling his past missteps into positive action.

As word of his advocacy spread, the school principal approached Nathan with a proposal: to speak at the upcoming school assembly, addressing the entire student body. Nathan accepted, recognizing the opportunity to make a significant impact.

The day of the assembly arrived, and the school gym was abuzz with anticipation. As Nathan stepped up to the podium, he took a moment to look out at the sea of faces before him—some curious, some skeptical, all waiting to hear what he had to say. He cleared his throat and began.

"Today, I want to share a personal story with you," Nathan started, his voice steady and clear. "It's about something that happened to me because of the decisions I made online. Decisions that I thought were harmless but ended up putting me and my family in danger."

Nathan detailed how his friendship with what he thought was a fellow gamer turned into a nightmare. He explained how sharing seemingly innocent information led to identity theft, financial loss, and emotional distress. He described the feeling of betrayal and the long, arduous process of reclaiming his and his family's security.

"But I learned something very important," Nathan continued. "Our actions online have real-world consequences. We need to be aware of the information we share, who we're sharing it with, and how it can be used against us."

The room was silent, every student absorbed in Nathan's every word, understanding the gravity of his experience.

"I'm not here to tell you to stop using the internet. It's a great tool, but like any tool, we need to use it responsibly. I want to encourage you to think about your privacy, to be cautious and to help protect not just yourself but your friends and family."

Nathan concluded with a call to action, encouraging his fellow students to become advocates for their own safety by staying informed and vigilant.

As he stepped down from the podium, the applause was loud and supportive. Students approached him afterward, thanking him for sharing his story, and teachers commended his bravery and maturity.

Nathan walked out of the gym feeling a mixture of relief and accomplishment. He had turned his ordeal into a powerful message, one that resonated with others, hopefully enough to inspire change. He knew the digital world would continue to evolve, possibly presenting new threats, but he also knew he was better equipped to face them, and now, so were his peers.

Epilogue

In the dense outskirts of Guayaquil, Ecuador, a warehouse stood isolated, an anonymous structure among many, cloaked by the heavy drapes of twilight. Inside, shadows stretched across the concrete floor as the echo of approaching footsteps grew louder. A team of federal agents, clad in tactical gear, quietly surrounded the premises, communicating through subtle hand signals and whispered commands.

The lead agent, a grizzled veteran with keen eyes, motioned towards the entrance. With a swift, coordinated movement, the team breached the warehouse doors, flooding the dim interior with the harsh light from their flashlights.

"Clear!" one agent called out, sweeping the main floor. Boxes of computer parts and tangled wires were stacked haphazardly against the walls, but no sign of human presence. The team moved systematically, their senses alert for any hint of the quarry they had been hunting for months: Wade Allen Burgess.

As the agents cleared the main area, a faint humming sound drew their attention to a door at the back of the warehouse. With a hand signal, two agents approached, one readying his weapon while the other carefully opened the door.

The room beyond was small, barely more than a closet, but what it contained sent a ripple of tension through the team. A lone computer setup, still running, its screens aglow with vibrant colors and figures moving in a digital world. The agents stepped closer, their eyes drawn to the figure on the screen—a character in the online game Craftworld, unmistakably dressed in a red shirt and blue jeans, the avatar of Nicodemus74.

One agent, trained in cyber forensics, sat down at the keyboard, his fingers moving quickly to secure any data that could lead them to Burgess. As he worked, the avatar on the screen began to dance, an eerie representation of defiance and mockery.

The room was otherwise empty, the only sounds the clicking of the keyboard and the soft hum of the computer. It was clear that Burgess had been tipped off, leaving behind only the barest trace of his presence—a digital ghost dancing in a world of his own creation.

"Looks like he knew we were coming," the lead agent muttered, frustration lining his face as he surveyed the room. The setup was sophisticated, indicating that Burgess had been operating from this location for some time, possibly coordinating his illicit activities across the globe.

Despite the setback, the discovery of the computer provided a new vein of information. The forensics team collected the hard drives and any other potential evidence, hopeful that it would eventually lead them to Burgess.

As the agents prepared to leave, the screen flickered before going dark, the dancing avatar disappearing into the digital ether. They stepped out into the night, the air thick with the promise of rain and the unresolved tension of the chase.

Back at their local field office, the data from the warehouse would be analyzed, each byte dissected for clues. The pursuit of Wade Allen

Burgess would continue, the agents driven by the knowledge that somewhere out there, the man who hid behind Nicodemus74 was already planning his next move.

About the Author

Michael-Paul Huling is a native of Rhode Island and now resides peacefully in the Quiet Corner of Connecticut with his beautiful wife and children that inspire him to do better every day. He's been writing stories, poetry, and songs for as long as he's been able to.

MICHAEL-PAUL HULING

www.ingramcontent.com/pod-product-compliance
Lightning Source LLC
LaVergne TN
LVHW051628050326
832903LV00033B/4707